_hydrus

Copyright © 2021 Hydrus
Cover Copyright © 2021 Hydrus

All rights reserved.

The characters depicted in this book are fictitious. Any similarity to real persons, living or dead, is coincidental and not intended by the author.

The scanning, uploading, and distribution of this book without permission is a theft of the author's intellectual property. If you would like permission to use material from the book (other than for review purposes), please contact hydruspoetry@gmail.com. Thank you for your support of theauthor's rights.

Published by: Hydrus
Photography by: Hydrus
Cover Design by: Cleo Moran - Devoted Pages Designs
Cover IStockphoto (Raven head): Tristan Wedgbury
Formatting by: Cleo Moran - Devoted Pages Designs
https://www.devotedpages.com

Manufactured in the United States of America

ISBN: 978-1-7357824-5-4

I live in death so that life can wait for me in the end.

_hydrus

Dedicated to those of us
who cannot avoid living life in the shadows

ENDthology is a collection of poems drawn up from experiences, thoughts, and emotions. Not everything in the world is dark, but many times we live without any light. We lose ourselves in what we consider our reality. Our souls forget what is important. At the same time, we rejoice when we regain our passion and our inner light.

Our mortal journey consists of loving all things that bring us joy. What we consider meaningful, valuable, and sacred. It also deals with the pain of losing things that we cherish. Especially the loss of those we hold dear to our hearts on earth and beyond. Life can be erotic in its way and curiously twisted. Not everything needs to be explained or have a blueprint to just be.

It is a constant struggle between the temptations of right and wrong. What we consider good versus what others may consider evil. The little voices in our head that tease and taunt us. Battles with the mind and our condition. Labels and finger-pointing and the stresses of responsibility. Its made up of quiet highs and darkened lows. Our journey is a paradox of feelings and contradictions. A fluid abyss of trying to be found when we are always feeling so very lost.

Yet in all its darkness there is always hope. A hope that we all control. It is a choice we all must make to be who we are. An unconditional decision to love ourselves. In that self-love there are no mistakes, there is only our unique journey. One that we must travel without self-judgment. That will always be relentlessly evolving and tirelessly changing. You have the gift to make your own choice.

We might live many lives, but which one will you always remember?

What memories will we ink? What will have true meaning? How will we live our END?

There is no End

just a very far beginning

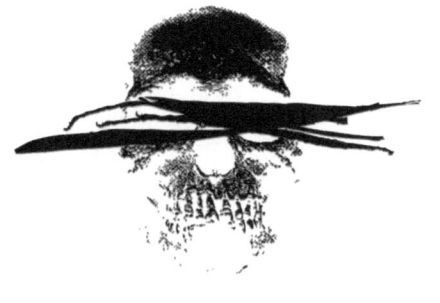

Heavens arms
Slowly turn
In the grains of sand
We barely learn
Each action lived
All seconds past
Trust in yourself
The start ends fast

Stages
_hydrus

Winds are silent
Thoughts are vague
Visions blur
Where you laid

Sadness clouds
Obscures all feel
Darkness veils
What is real

Memories sink
Dreams survive
Nothing to think
When did I die

Questions
_hydrus

Secret illusions
Cloud my nights
Strained temptations
Haunt the light
Intimate pleasures
Disguised allure
Committed relations
Objectively pure
Implied affections
Plague intent
Obscure delusions
Masked repent
Shameful perception
Fraudulent path
Innocence scorned
Malicious the wrath

Awake
_hydrus

Enchanted message
Recoiled thoughts
Triggered feelings
Puzzled wants

Annoyed seduction
Games are played
Simple answers
Obsessed ways

Feed the tempted
Reap the few
Peeved fixation
Charmed recluse

Excited dreamer
Unknown faith
Alarmed intentions
Humbled disgrace

Plummet
_hydrus

Elusive feelings
Cautious tales
Heartfelt visions
Discreet spells
Hidden secrets
Loaded grin
Subdued glances
Sensual skin
Pressing flesh
Mounted moans
Ardent tastes
Fervent groans
Whispered words
Forgotten times
Missing moments
Wish you were mine

Confession
_hydrus

Unthinkable the notion
Ones vision would be blurred
Drunken in the moment
Unintelligibly slurred

Wondrous attraction
Conveniently mused
Sightless affiliation
Masked in abuse

Inexplicable stranger
Cloaked to conceive
Ripped from my womb
My son was deceived

Calculated
_hydrus

A thousand tears
Could never say
How I felt
When you went away

Such emptiness
Devoured my soul
Sadness lived
And took its control

My love my all
Had left my side
Torn from me
Too fast to fight

A broken shell
Was left in sand
To never feel
That warmth again

Shattered life
Choices made
Another day
Has slipped away

Your words in me
Hum like songs
Reminders of right
And so many wrongs

Distant whispers
With silly smiles
Memories awake
The infantile

In me your flame
Will forever burn
Lessons taught
Nothing learned

Until we meet
On a crowded beach
Pain will sit
And I will reach

So Much
_hydrus

Don't only matter
when someone else decides
you matter

_hydrus

Shivers kindle
Tempted itch
Lurking fingers
Hidden twitch
Lapping tongue
Tip ignites
Gentle strokes
Sweetened bites
Anxious veins
Fuel to sip
Muscles beat
Painted lips

Rush
_hydrus

Wailing calls
Search in fear
Grasping claws
Pull me near
Hallowed screams
Leave their scent
Gruesome deeds
Dark intent
Sifting screeches
Hungry howls
Eager footsteps
Wretched growls
Famished beasts
Shadowed shapes
Mauling nightmare
No escape

Chased
_hydrus

Those who challenge you
Fear that you already won

_hydrus

Buried beneath
Broken walls
Collapsed
By earth and tears
Extinguished passion
Flightless loss
My ashes
Have turn to fear

Gone
_hydrus

Chained to an empty tale
Life has withered in rain
Lost without serenitys sail
Misguided by my dismal pain

Adrift Again
_hydrus

Ambitious battle fought
Fervors courage claimed
Grim emotions rot
Ceaseless burning strain

Glory is the beaten
Corpses dance on bones
Red crossed horizon
Barren muffled drones

Weakness will be buried
Hopeless is the fight
Repressed hostile feelings
Ruthless rage unites

Lethal
_hydrus

Spilled thread of pain
Dampens lonesome sheet
Stipples turn the brain
Turmoil temps defeat

Sharpened lead slices
Tortured thoughts scream
Anguished sacrifices
Deranged drafted dreams

Crude jagged scribbles
Harness every fear
Disgusted leaves shrivel
Exploited lines smear

Failures vainly teach
Swallowed flaws sink
Ramblings beaten screech
Shaken streams ink

Torn
_hydrus

Streaks of sin
Paint her face
Blackened leather
Fiery lace
Steel and chain
Adorn her cage
Pain to play
Embedded rage
Deceptive huntress
Teasing ways
Seduced Temptation
Born to slay

Fearless
_hydrus

Nightmares interrupted
Madness concealed
Deluded the visions
Malevolence so real

Hooked are the talons
That feast on my soul
Exploiting my kindness
Ceasing control

Disturbed the solution
One that I crave
Slicing its head
Digging its grave

For reapers do sleep
Darkness heeds will
Some secrets I keep
Kindness will kill

Carve
_hydrus

Faith saves even those who defy it

_hydrus

Wounded existence
Eroding my flesh
Erased as a failure
Disguised in neglect

Depleting the light
All aspects went dark
Enraged with seclusion
Punctured the spark

Turmoil left vacant
Stubbornly grim
Living without her
All due to him

Confined
_hydrus

Life has made us broken
but we still cherish the pieces we keep
_hydrus

Abandoned corpse
I carry home
On my back
Still all alone

It cannot rest
Or grieve today
My burdened life
Wont go away

Shadow
_hydrus

Dark lit room
Engulfs our shapes
Tender kisses
Slowly trace

Wondering eyes
Captured trance
Hidden pleasures
Starved romance

Escape we must
Lies to place
Our hearts we trust
Leave no trace

A life together
Fates our plan
Lets disappear
To start again

Runaway
_hydrus

Sunlight pierces
Tainted glass
Morning meadows
Winding path

Through tall grasses
I catch your eye
Hollowed oaks
Still survive

Engraved affairs
A distant past
What once was
Could never last

Thoughts of you
Still live in me
Departed angels
Sweet symphony

Winds
_hydrus

Tragic castaway
Unbridled muse
Mistaken contempt
Flaws confused

Unwavering want
Regretful advance
Distinctive in nature
Obsessive the trance

Lustful intentions
Intimate touch
Savage the mishaps
Undesirable crush

Hunted with reason
Left without chase
Useless my vision
Frenzied disgrace

Unwanted
_hydrus

Heads erupt
As the anvils crash
Imploding skulls
Severed and thrashed
Eager minstrels
Pull the strings
Oddly grimace
Who will win
Divine justice
Hands can't wait
Titillated
By lifes fate
Tender beings
Naive to drink
Actions happen
Not as you think

Foolish
_hydrus

Your heart will answer what your mind questions.
_hydrus

Nagging disturbance
Battering thoughts
Persistent intrusions
Withered distraught

Audible demons
Perched on my mind
Plaguing so common
Harassment refined

Constant the badger
Twisted the means
Always deceiving
Intrusively keen

Laughter and banter
Hushes quite small
Echoes betray me
They wait for my fall

Murmurs
_hydrus

Toxic loathing
Stings to squirm
Heartbeat splinters
Slowly it burns

Inflicted strikes
Numbs to the touch
Ingested malice
Morphing in lust

Vipers kisses
Tempts with sweets
Unaware hisses
Tainted such heat

Seductive fury
Baits the lair
A coiled delusion
Eaten rare

Twisted
_hydrus

Sirens dance
In dripping salt
A drowning trance
Seductions cult

Petrels beg
Drowning flight
Waves that thrash
Virgins delight

Few which dare
Fight the tide
Lances bare
Forbidden ride

Hunters gather
Spears in hand
Mapped desires
Forbidden lands

Fated cast
None will save
Unholy mast
Tridents rage

Vanished
_hydrus

In silence
The monsters play
Eating all
Our thoughts away
What cannot be seen
One will think
Poisoned images
We quickly drink
May all the noise
Just cease to be
Return me to
Tranquility

Chatter
_hydrus

Savage the stare
That tempts my heart
Yearning a touch
A kiss to start
One touch to follow
Lips to seal
Wonders imagined
Thirsting so real

Desired
_hydrus

Surrender and
love yourself first

Light the flames that
will scorch the earth

You are feared
because you are unstoppable

No one understands your needs
until they have needs
—Hydrus

Hands stand still
Shadows loom
Melted ice sits
A dusty room

Moans are written
Wax has burned
Flesh once bitten
All marks earned

Bodies drenched
Hardened might
Twitching lips
Grips are tight

Heaven sleeps
Hearts still pound
Hunger reaps
Another round

Invitation
_hydrus

From the skies
I stealthily soar
Feasting eyes
Hunting evermore

Watching every
Fainted step
Lunging towards
All regrets

Tempted beak
Sharply shined
A fallen angel
So divine

Piercing screams
Scold the beast
Clouds erode
At his feet

Plunge
_hydrus

Judge my actions
Reflections trounce
Blade through throat
You I renounce

Stepped on chest
As you bleed
Severed saddle
Trampled stead

Drink your vanity
Watch me slay
Beheaded ego
Will end today

Instinct
_hydrus

Hallowed spaces
Filled with frantic cries
Demons whispers
Hint at my demise

Trusted voices
Rule my saddened nights
Regretful mornings
Buried in selfish lies

White Noise
_hydrus

Wounded mortal
Frail and bleak
Battered wings
Love you seek
In my arms
You belong
Heal in time
We can be strong

Fragile
_hydrus

Silence the Chaos

_hydrus

I woke up with empty hands now they hunger for something to feed
_hydrus

Spirits return
To simply take
Bleeding hearts
They gorge to taste

Buried brains
Dripped in song
Putrid visions
Morbidly hung

Maggots dressed
In sundays flesh
Rotting in
Octobers best

A place has been
Dug for me
Where the flies
Inside conceive

Rest
_hydrus

A sun that rises and never fades
An endless horizon with crashing waves
Thunderous clouds and heavy rains
All the worlds joy and endless pain
Apologetic love that lives on
Unconditional rights to all of my wrongs
Stern in stance and gracious might
Quick to guide and hold me tight
Nothing can compare to this
A heart that I will always miss

Eternal
_hydrus

Midnight lifts
As neon blinks
Smokey mist paints
Ink filled wrists

Stares of lust
Lace whiskey sips
Tongues that lap
Thirst for drips

Moments pass
Hands reach their mark
Tracing lines
Plunge in the dark

Muscles tense
A stranger's kiss
Seductive secrets
Uncover bliss

Motive
_hydrus

Serpents dwell
As the casket rots
Ravens flock
To perch their spots

Looted bones
Pillaged schemes
Savage swarms
Trampled dreams

Lifeless theft
Tearful lies
Evils left
Spirits dies

Spoils
_hydrus

Shattered world
Broken heart
King of pieces
Torn apart

Inconsolable
A total mess
Lost in darkness
Full of regrets

In this moment
All were ghosts
Full of wisdom
None were close

Heavy fog
A distant shape
Came to save
New found escape

When all fled
You buried in
Brought me close
From within

Provided hope
So I could rise
Now we cope
To feel alive

Resurrected
_hydrus

Every
conversation
with myself
ends
up in
silence

_hydrus

Fractured mortality
Severed existence
Ripped from birth

Imperfect reality
Impaired survival
Splintered worth

Confused seclusion
Frightful society
Masked in fear

Breached biology
Ruptured humanity
Fate not clear

Uncertain
_hydrus

Tempted whispers
Sing their kiss
Dark intentions
Blissful wish

Silent chatter
Oddly seeks
Pensive banter
Never sleeps

Words are dormant
Hellhounds wane
Idle suffering
Slumbers pain

Eyes impaled
Fires reign
Tortured calm
Thoughts are slain

Rest
_hydrus

Lavish petals
Dipped in wine
Tender tulips
Tangled vines

Hinted scents
Arousing charm
Hidden motives
Raised to harm

Dire bloom
Sprouted scorn
Nurtured loom
Uncoiled thorns

Seed
_hydrus

Marks dress our throats
As the broken ropes dance
Red lights hummed
An intoxicated trance

Leather draped walls
Painted on skin
Wet stained lips
Sweat filled sin

Cracking whips kneel
Thick etched air
Eyes remain feeding
Salivating stares

Flavored embers burn
Hungers persist
New pages turn
Only we exist

Impulse
_hydrus

I long all day
To reach my nights
Just to dream
A captured sight

One glimpse is all
A kiss or touch
Brief the moment
Ferventing rush

A warm embrace
The subtle smile
Tender words
Some juvenile

Blurry notes
That sadness sings
Whispered tears
Angelic wings

Among all mist
Grief still awaits
Ironic twist
Never to awake

Shutter
_hydrus

I dont
Recognize
My reflection
Its empty stare
Ignores
My memory

_hydrus

Hidden brutality
Unearthed from birth
Unseen mortality
Degraded worth

Questionable doubts
Malice with hate
Concealing the shouts
Backhands irate

Blood befriends broken
Bruises decorate flesh
Silence not spoken
Skin carved and etched

Suffering my manifest
Maimed tears are bled
Panic plagues the chest
Heart severed from head

Sculpted
_hydrus

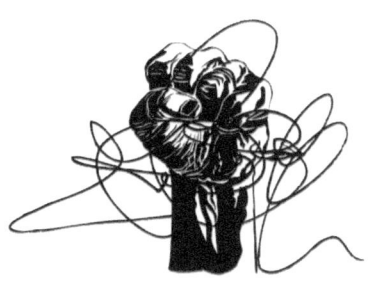

Bones that never batter
Nor metal that pierced blue
Shields made for protection
Guillotines of the few

A single breath made silent
Humanities tainted gasp
Outrage veiled in sadness
He will not be the last

When will we learn

Cries
_hydrus

Outstretched arms
Carved in swine
Ribcage gorged
Split intertwined
Hanging skin
Draped to bleed
Hidden smirks
Hide misdeeds
Crimson hues
Rain from the skies
Umbrellas speak
Of suicide
No one sleeps
As the time grows near
All will watch
Gasp in fear
Hollow martyrs
A clenching test
Humanities ghost
Laid to rest

Francis Bacon
_hydrus

A mangled corpse
Lays on my bed
Bloodied pillows
Shattered head

Sheets that dress
Knotted, tied
Tattered mess
Consumed lies

Seductive deeds
Splattered floors
Forbidden needs
Nevermore

At a glimpse
Peace has come
Flies appear
We are done

Fraud
_hydrus

Blackened feathers
Drape my soul
Sharpened talons
Caged control

Purple hues
Fired in flesh
Sliced and bruised
Words are wept

Tears now sharpened
Tongues refined
Betrayed audition
Love declined

Hooded virtue
Wounded flame
Masked intrusion
Unholy shame

Shrouded
_hydrus

She dripped when I saw her
and I drank until she left

_hydrus

Tiled walls smeared in mold
Tell of tales never told

Droplets scrape to wash all fear
Tinted fingers stained to smear

Abrasive scrub impales distaste
Abstract removal of wretched waste

Buried caverns in pipes roam
Drowning blood soaked in foam

Flooded feelings echo pain
Innocence lost inside a drain

Foul
_hydrus

Lost moments
I forgot to tell
So unforgettable
A blurry hell

One cant remember
Pained omissions past
Where dreams befriended
And would never last

No memory
_hydrus

Broken glass
Blood stained floors
Shattered windows
Unhinged doors

Rummaged trash
Ripped up clothes
A hidden monster
No one knows

Blank
_hydrus

Winter snarls
Rejoice in sin
Chained screams
Kept within
Voices taunt
Replay our loss
Tempting demons
At what cost
Broken pieces
Never mend
Soulless species
Just pretend
Hollow happiness
Empty pledge
Saddened smokestacks
On the edge

Questioned
_hydrus

Banished torment
Abducted eyes
Cruel defiance
Demoralized
Devils mischief
You accuse
Unrelenting
Hangmans muse
Just a servant
Scribbling lies
Worthless wanderer
Vilified
An empty compass
Tongues are cut
Ravens vanish
Cleansed to rot

Uncut
_hydrus

Love does not define time
Pain remembers every second
_hydrus

Wastelands surround
Emptiness contained
Drained corruption
Games unexplained

Teased by temptation
Aroused in fear
Cursed manipulations
Footsteps grow near

Anticipation looms
Forgotten the fog
Abundant defiance
Lost is the cause

Weeping in shadows
Matches burn breath
Mourning the shackles
Devotion in death

Requiem
_hydrus

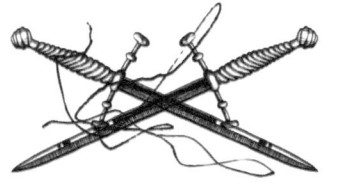

Embedded the dagger
Found simply in place
Ironic the gesture
Sinful distaste
Perjured intention
Avarice conceived
Self serving the pleasure
Twisted to bleed

Scab
_hydrus

I was blinded
By a world of grief
The unwilling pardon
Of a loves deceit

In its absence
I burned my faith
My misfortunes
Will be my grave

Casket
_hydrus

Broken the anchor
That sinks in the storm
Tangled in chains
Its wrecks it adorns

A reluctant escape
To the depths of all life
The meaningless thrill
Of a timely delight

Futile
_hydrus

I found heaven in your hell

Twisted
_hydrus

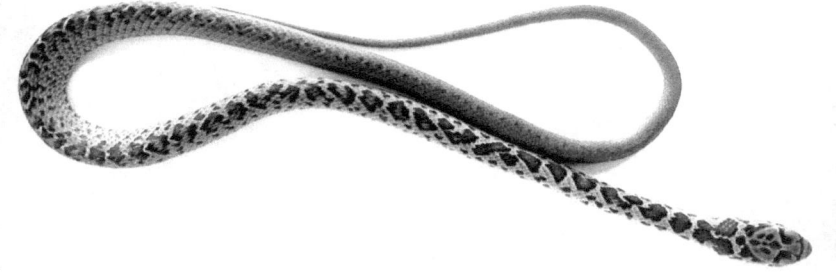

The love you took from me
Lives silently in the tears
You mistake for your own

Serpent
_hydrus

Spectres tease
Drape my sight
Stirring panic
Hades delight

Morbid bait
Sadistic groans
Casted fates
Followed home

Mauling calls
Purring chills
Suspects stalk
Tempted thrills

Absent voices
Taunt and claw
Unspoken noises
Summon all

Visited
_hydrus

A cage without bars
In a broken mirror you stare
Threading needles through scars
Reflections mock the unclear

Jagged are the tools
Carved out by your desire
Sculpting such illusions
Smiths posing as liars

Worlds sketched in alleys
Spirits smudged for fame
Convenient all the falsehoods
Penciled in made up pain

Inscription
_hydrus

Candles burn
As the whispers fade
Our love laid down
In its shallow grave
Hopeless actions
Try to reanimate
A rejected soul
In its battered state
Life has left
All the joy has cast
Shoveled soils
Filling the past
Lasting quiet
Until the mourning crow
Reviving memories
Of the pain you know

Dormant
_hydrus

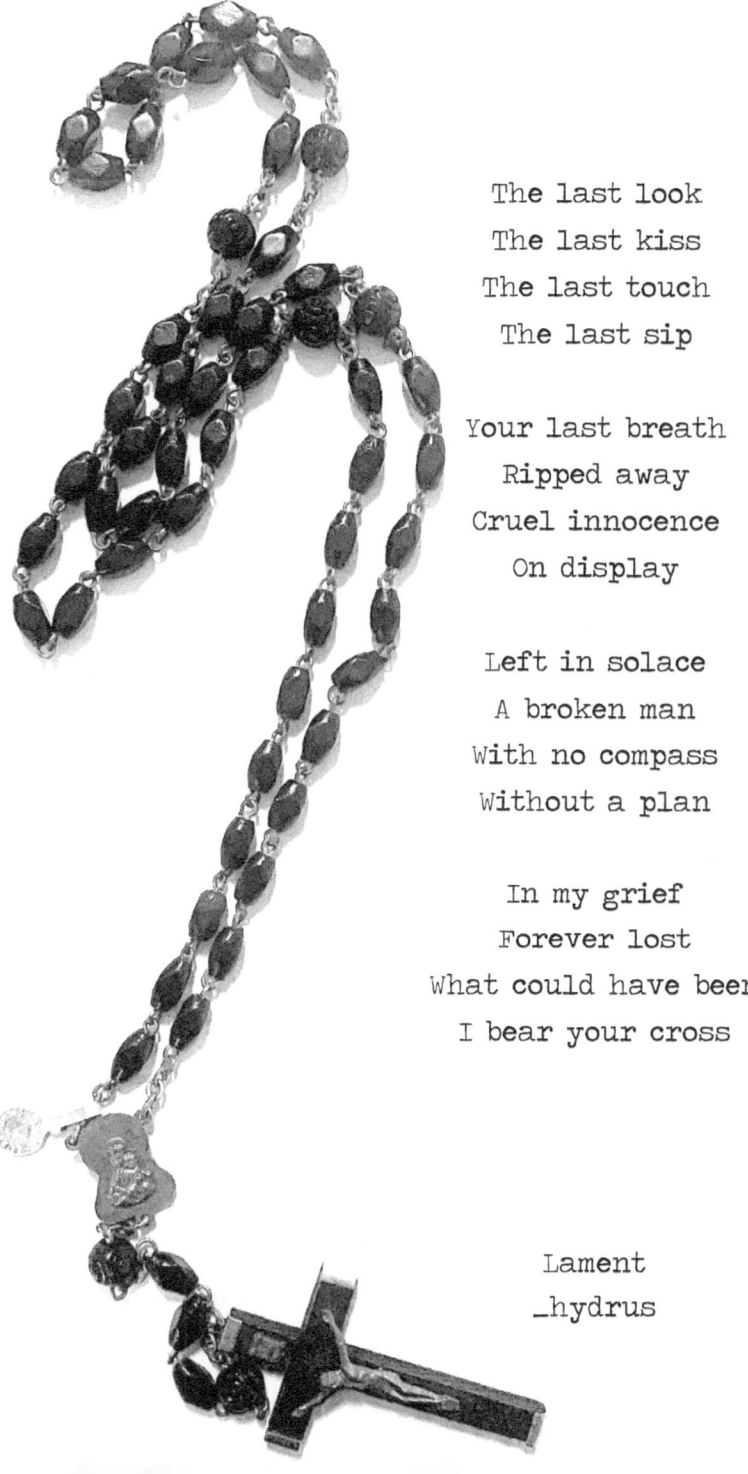

The last look
The last kiss
The last touch
The last sip

Your last breath
Ripped away
Cruel innocence
On display

Left in solace
A broken man
With no compass
Without a plan

In my grief
Forever lost
What could have been
I bear your cross

Lament
_hydrus

Splintered hands bleed
Upon my own chest
Crushed quiet sleep
Monsters will undress

Guilt gropes rest
Kneeling needs paid
Wickedness confessed
Illusions waned away

Eroded
_hydrus

I will pick up my ashes

and hide them in the wind.

_hydrus

In my blood
Quietly I stand
A painted symphony
Crimson hands

Eyes closed
Drenched in your scent
Memories tasted
Full of descent

Sedated life
Innocence betrayed
Seized existence
All afraid

Wounded whimpers
Turn to growls
Patient vengeance
Fury howls

Fierce in fire
Revenge is swift
Silenced torment
My sinful gift

Serenity
_hydrus

In my thoughts
You resonate
Timeless guilt
Sinful taste

One more drip
Need to quench
Paint your lips
Build my trench

Here I lay
Blindly curled
Engulfed in passion
Missing my world

Absent dreams
Stalk all bliss
Replayed visions
A phantom kiss

Will you return
And understand
Start again
Take my hand

Complicated
_hydrus

Eyes open
Full of tears
Dreamt of us
Disappeared
One more visit
Haunt my light
Confined desires
Holding tight
Marks proclaim
All thats yours
Darkened pleasures
On your floor
Nights new shadow
Begs again
Captured passion
Knows no end

Crossing
_hydrus

Enraged hope
Crashing shores
Battered eyes
Unexplored
Wilted petals
Staggered frame
Disillusioned
Lashing reign
Toxic chalice
Hinted bliss
Venoms cauldron
Ornate hiss
Claws caressing
Witches see
Shadowed harpy
Cannot flee

Fed
_hydrus

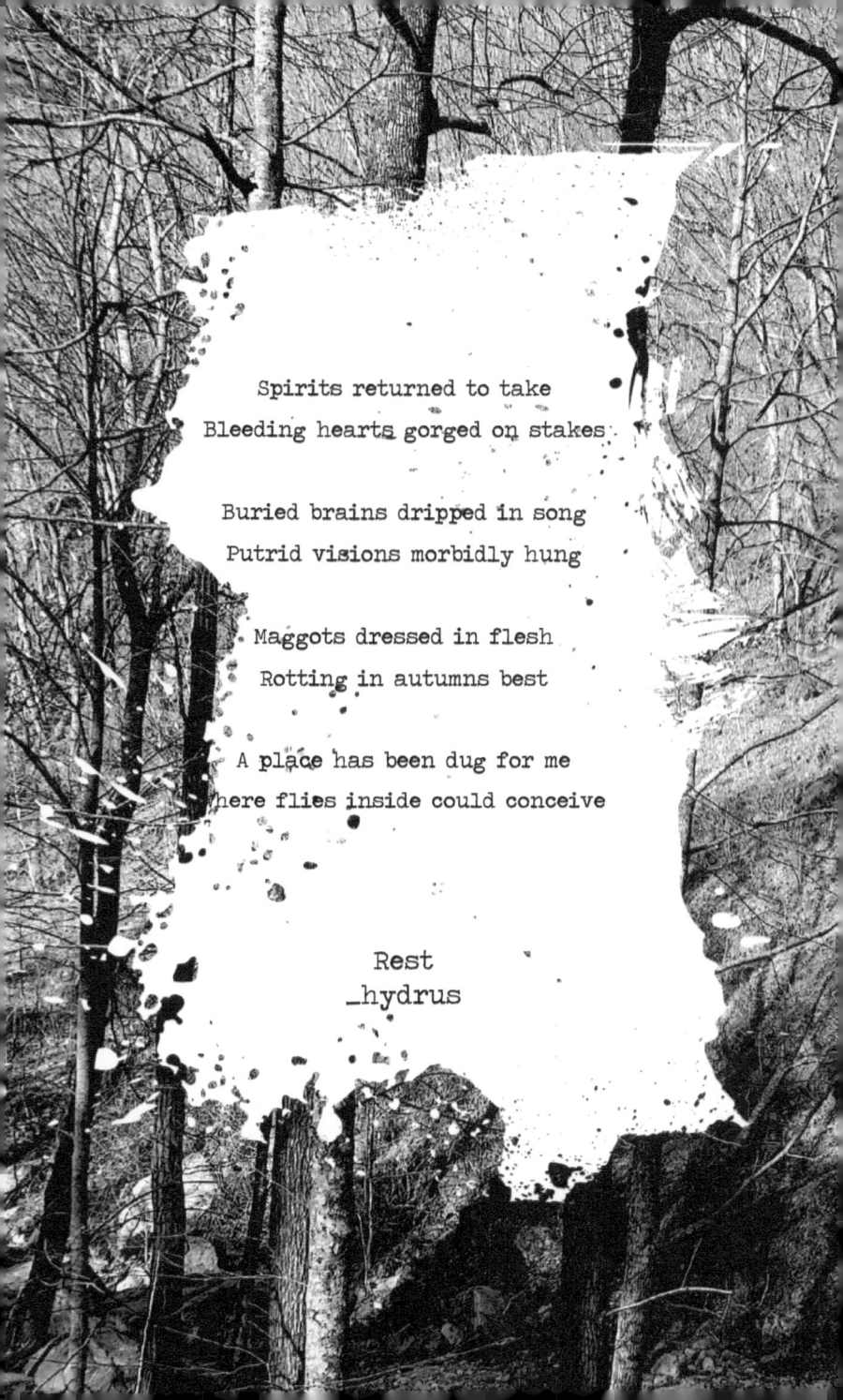

Spirits returned to take
Bleeding hearts gorged on stakes

Buried brains dripped in song
Putrid visions morbidly hung

Maggots dressed in flesh
Rotting in autumns best

A place has been dug for me
here flies inside could conceive

Rest
_hydrus

Idled monarch
Sanctioned flight
Clipped horizon
Forbidden might
Damaged angel
Broken will
Heavens tangle
Captured ill
Beauties envy
Mirrored spawn
Trapped encounter
Moonlit dawn
Forsaken light
Trampled grace
Uncovered fright
Ended chase

Caught
_hydrus

Enchanted creature with eyes of pearls
Coiled in beauty in a sinister world
Slaying victims with a wicked tongue
Wielding chants from the blackened sun

Silent spells supple lips will cast
Mislead souls tempt a fiery wrath
A bite so sweet to flame the fed
Temptress queen to her nest one led

Outstretched wings in grace ignite
Begging suitors in her shadowed flight
Desperate martyrs kneel in muddled lies
While horned dragons rule the ravaged sky

Seduced demons crawl quick to treat
Shallowed gifts placed at her taloned feet
Raptures lady controls the alluring drip
Captive chalice full of forbidden sips

Queen
_hydrus

Faraway cyphers call out in song
Cherubs musings try to string along
Quiverless banshees stake their claim
All are pious to dine on fame

Wine pours as they write the notes
Recalled conquests scribbled in quotes
Sinister minds composing as a pack
Insidious prophets planning their attack

Rules are recited scratched in stone
Knives are rallied sliced on hilted bone
Thorned persistence breach the walls
Solemn spaces are tombs for all

Scripted solace set in flame for the choir
Reviled assailants ripped apart desires
Orphaned spirits plead to protect the horde
A single note left to die by chord

Outro
_hydrus

Stalking the shallows
Digging up my breath
Sinking in existence
Submerged just to reflect

Baited fear entangles
Floating ghosts will cheer
Dwindled lights are strangled
Smothered wreck is near

Quietly forgotten
Splashing laughs are mute
Gripping to forgiveness
Regrets drink in the truth

Abyss
_hydrus

Morning awoke her soul
As my tongue
Retraced our night

_hydrus

Quietly I find you
Broken wings on my lap
A shoulder of illusion
Life simply turned its back

Endless voices chatter
Filling hearts with doubt
Unforgiving time elapses
Strangers tend to shout

Innocence erases
Conflict comes with ease
Struggle claims its genius
Anything to please

Faith in hope will conquer
Light will blind the dark
Mended flight awakens
Inside her is the spark

Revived
_hydrus

Marooned in thought
As my person quakes
Wedged in contradiction
Misguided by mistakes

Volumes will speak
Suffered in peace
Tales of contempt
Scavenged by defeat

Narratives evolve
Smears dine on tears
Embattled without cause
Spaces made unclear

Empty inward paths
Reflections undefined
Neglected by the past
Feelings lost in time

Seclusion
_hydrus

Bones that rattle
Drag on stone
Sensing screeching
Howling groans

Morbid entrails
Haggard reek
Dragging down
A bloodied street

Flies adorn
Ones sorrowed brow
Perished wisdom
Gruesome foul

Beating hearts
Wait to dine
Suckling veins
Pour like wine

Night will take
Few uttered words
Death awaits
None are heard

Reaping
_hydrus

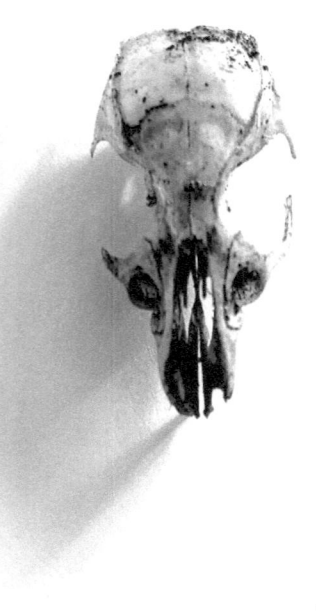

Forged sentiments
Gouge my stream
Imposed reflections
A charlatans dream

Hustled flavors
Tainted with scent
Impulsed deception
Preyed innocence

Uttered hoaxes
Destined to mate
Evoking your soul
As you contemplate

Moods are duped
Follow than flee
Fraudulent bards
Eager to feed

Unwavering tone
As wings flare away
Wicked intentions
Ravens will play

Thief
_hydrus

Storms beg as they crash in view
Frustration piloted by the drowning few

Devils murmur to breech your path
Eagerly plotting a merciless pact

Waves engorged with the sins of old
Twisting horizons as the shouts turn cold

Brawling afflictions nestled in sand
A dispirited struggle without demand

Combatant fury without will or sight
Ignited by falsehoods to their delight

Fallen angels have enraged the sea
A sightless course full of emptied pleas

Depleted resistance the depths now own
Adrift in his solace a voiceless home

Exile
_hydrus

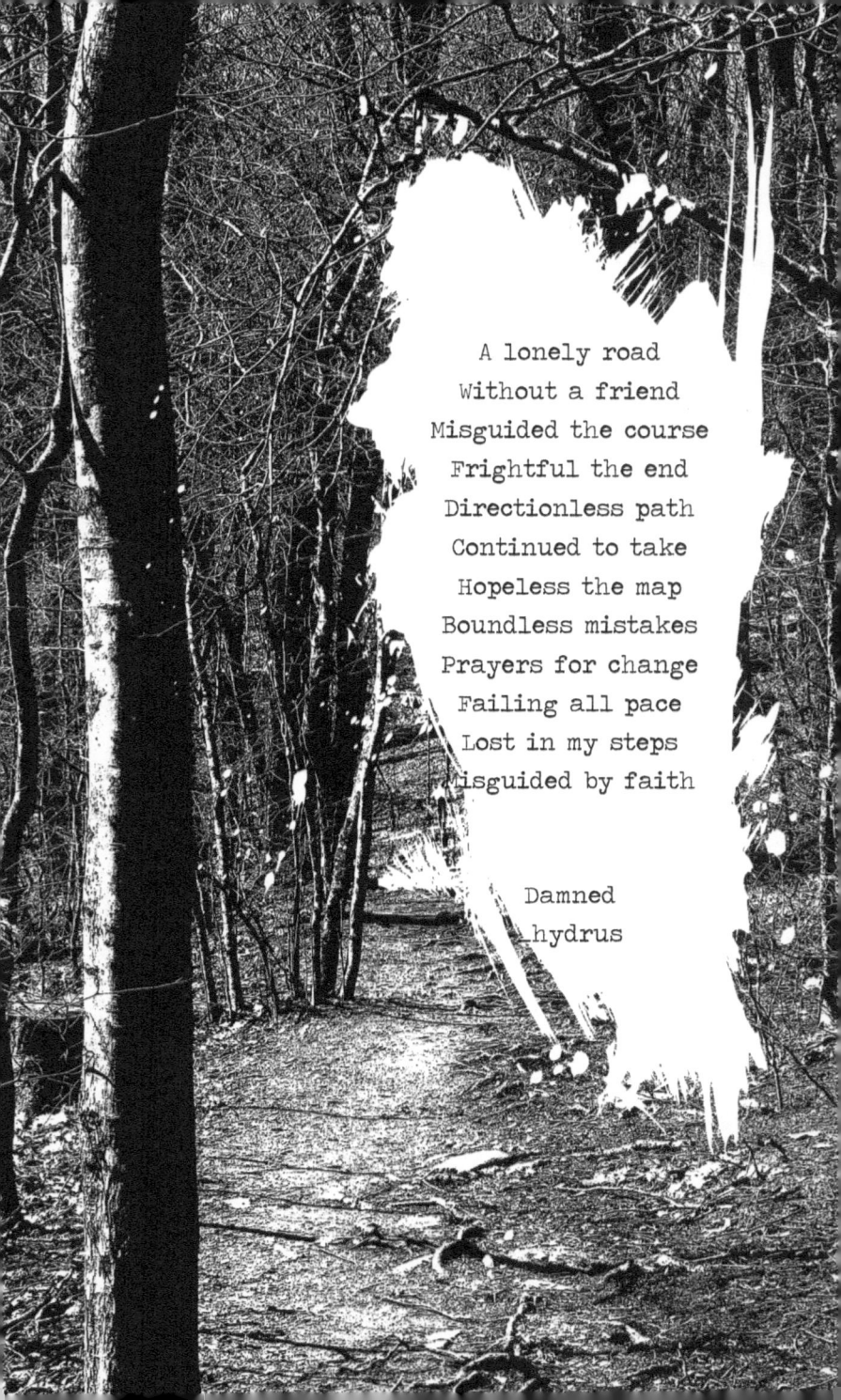

A lonely road
Without a friend
Misguided the course
Frightful the end
Directionless path
Continued to take
Hopeless the map
Boundless mistakes
Prayers for change
Failing all pace
Lost in my steps
Misguided by faith

Damned
hydrus

Black veil
Towers over me
Consuming my
Living effigy
Hopeless thoughts
Mimic signs
Unlock sorrow
So redefined
Will these shadows
Blend away
Or simply taunt
To keep all grey

Muted
_hydrus

You drowned me

to save your soul

_hydrus

Screaming skulls in a gallows wail
Mounted throats as the pain exhales
Convicted fortune of a lonely thief
Sliced iron against his crushing teeth

Soulless skins adorn a bloodied plank
Branded nomad without Gods to thank
Mangled horror displayed angst to please
Nourishing hunger for a voyeurs tease

Hands stretch out from the foraged herds
Exclaiming hexes in enchanted words
A single kindling of a witched pyre
Birthed the seed of an unclaimed fire

Averse witness heart etched to strike
Concealed engagement born of the night
Obscured betrayal now masked to kill
Avenging the name to revoke the thrill

Slain existence is a judgments shame
Combusted lies in a corrupt game
Seething flames will engulf the caster
As ravens gorge and consume the master

Vendetta
_hydrus

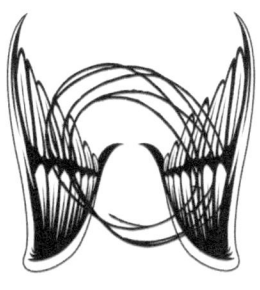

Each day grows darker
As the sun shines for all
I dreamed of a whisper
That started my fall

Touched by my angel
An invisible kiss
Memories are my penance
My endless abyss

Lost
_hydrus

Battled temptations
Wielding its form
Allured entrapment
Seduced to transform

Wicked the mental
Preys on the weak
Hunting in splendor
Searching to peak

Waiting in corners
Knives of the dead
Quietly bedding
To slice off his head

Many the pleasure
Taken in spite
Watching the hunted
Die with delight

Baited
_hydrus

Reach for what is yours...
Its inside you
    _hydrus

As you approach
Something in me dies
Transfixed on your stench
Strangled by your lies

Your mouth wreaks of flesh
Swatted by the flies
A tangled tongue inspects
Internally I cry

Wretched sins infest
Watching as you dine
Poisons will ingest
Swallowed with your wine

Now the tainted glass
Nestles you to sleep
Gladly you will pass
Intoxicated thief

Waste
_hydrus

You really do not remember
The way you killed my soul
Methodically deceiving
Establishing control

A flaw in your perfection
Brutal with your hands
Destructively demeaning
Abusive with demands

Time became an ally
Bad habits foretold your fate
Power was relinquished
Your hostage became irate

Will and might took over
Fear engulfed the frail
Battered skull slumped over
Justice hammered nail

Switch
_hydrus

A broken compass
Plagues my heart
Misdirected
Far from love
Path misguided
Lost my way
No more chances
Castaway

Astray
_hydrus

In her tears I captured the reality
That I was not worth causing them
Much less holding them

Truth
_hydrus

I lost you when I opened up my heart
Only to realize you could not
Repair how broken I was
Now I am in pieces

Ripped Open
_hydrus

A sadness haunts
My every breath
Of moments lost
New found regrets
Words that were
Never said
But always felt
Forever meant
What could have been
Was not to be
Our love became
The enemy

Sorrow
_hydrus

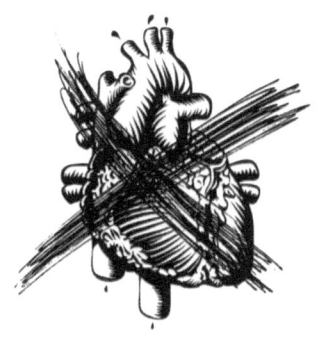

My loneliness began the moment
I knew we could never be together

And my heart had become a part of you
That I could never let go

Never
_hydrus

Rains ignored my pain
Sadness cried in every drop
In my hands lay the screams
This storm will never stop

Reflections in my wounds
Broken as I drown
Waiting for the tide to rise
To erase my every sound

Dissolved
_hydrus

Barren stares
Claims their pose
Blackened sun
A blood dripped rose

Burning wounds
Left not to heal
Betrayed emotions
Confessed ordeal

Now they lay
Twisted seeds
Unknown remorse
Drowned in deeds

A chance was taken
Mistakes were made
Accused deception
Enraged escape

Sentenced
_hydrus

Bury me
Knowing that
I will always
Love you

_hydrus

Only the light from your heart
Can illuminate the love I have for you in darkness
Without you I simply fade

Disappearing
_hydrus

Feelings of guilt
Burdening thoughts
A lost horizon
Unclaimed for love

All was given
Happiness pursued
When one was needed
Selfish acts ensued

Choices made
As the rains passed
Unkept promises
Nothing asked

Contemplation
What could have been
Why you were gone
Still haunts within

Too Late
_hydrus

The death in me awakes
When your tears pour on to me
Stars lose life when I feel your sorrow
I retreat inside to keep myself hidden
My heart lives for your quiet breath
Thoughts of you blend into my soul
If only you were mine I could exist

Boundless
_hydrus

Pressed against the wall
Drowning in our sweat
With each moaning breath
Our destiny was met

_hydrus

It is hard to stay awake
When you only live in sleep
A place we call our own
Where reality ceases to be

I wish my eyes would not open
For this is where you breathe
An everlasting slumber
A love that will never leave

Together
_hydrus

The sun has fallen
Never to return
Casting a final light
One final turn

All that waits
Is the saddened moon
Helpless in space
Gone way too soon

Starless
_hydrus

Only a shadow can
Capture her trace
A vanished whisper that
Winds interlace
The rustling leaves
Swaying in air
Ones distant thoughts
Wake us so near
Faraway laughter
Hurts with each laugh
Still echoes all
Dormant and passed
Beats breathed without
Having a chance
Discovering you and never
Feeling true romance

Gone
_hydrus

A taste on a finger
Has left me in chains
Caged in delusions
Trapped by your game

Lusting to have you
Wrapped in my sweat
Covered and tracing
Leashed as your pet

Marked is the skin
Delivered to eat
Waiting commands
Nocturnal the beast

When you arrive
In seclusion I wait
Eager the binge
Surrendered as bait

Served
_hydrus

The Outline
You left in my bed
Screams at me
Taunts my existence
Your void
Is deafening
An unbearable absence
Tormented
Without your breath
Yet haunted
By your deletion
Lost within myself
Abandoned
To be forgotten

Numb
_hydrus

Your dose of reality
Ruined the fantasy
No longer caged in a game
I live for vengeance

Warned
_hydrus

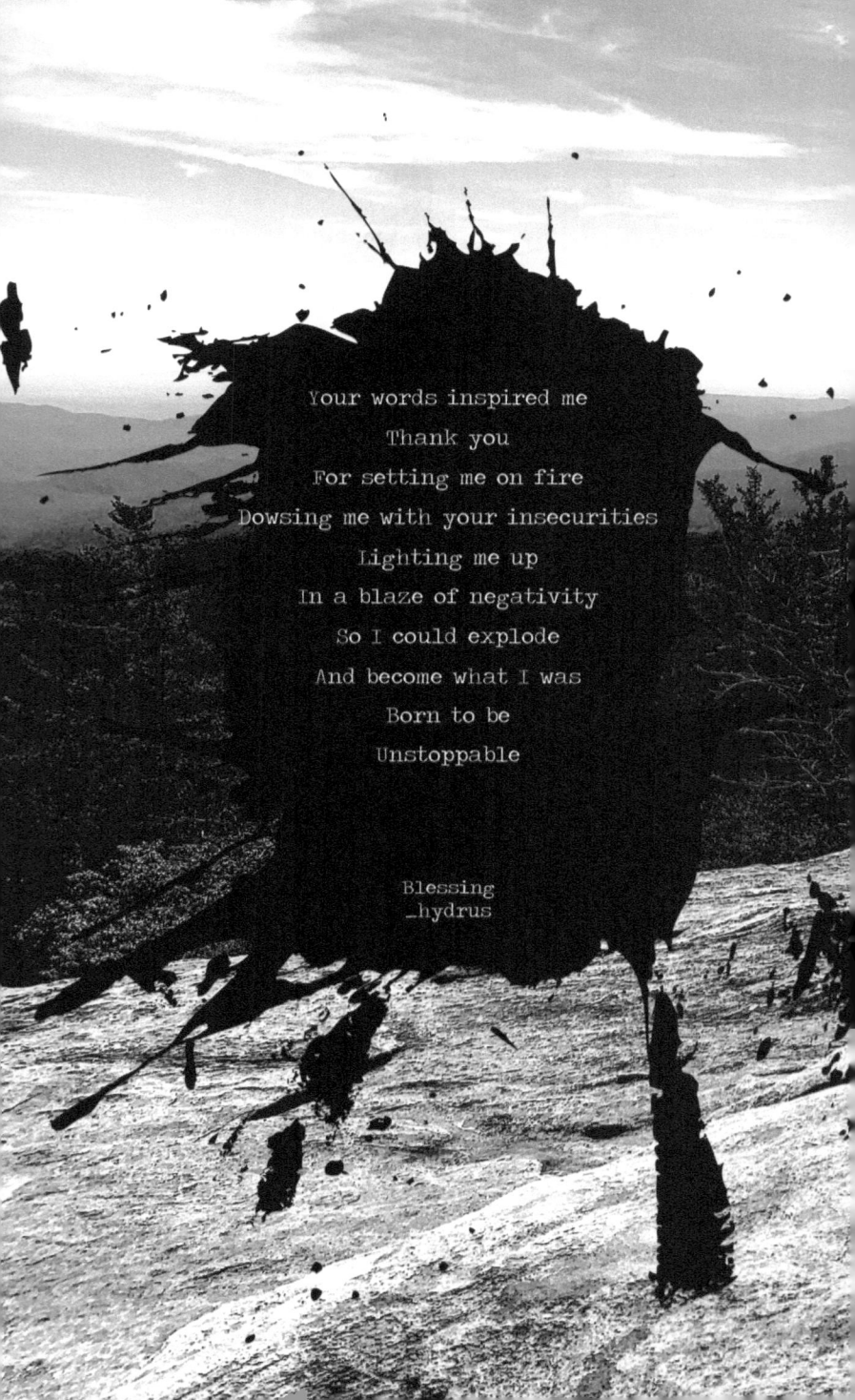

Your words inspired me
Thank you
For setting me on fire
Dowsing me with your insecurities
Lighting me up
In a blaze of negativity
So I could explode
And become what I was
Born to be
Unstoppable

Blessing
_hydrus

In the shadows you will fly
A confessed remorseful site
Your colors pray and plead
For the answers to ignite

Inked are your wings
Majestically sincere
Dark sweet angel
Life is just unclear

My black butterfly
Muted as you glide
Defiant in your flight
So beautifully alive

Never once held
Only to be seen
Wondrous creature lives
Unworthy of a dream

Pinned
_hydrus

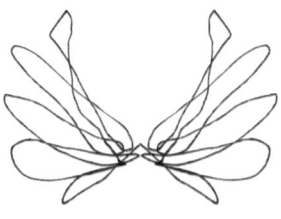

Your love became my horizon
Until shallow waters
Eclipsed my fall

Separated
_hydrus

Ablaze
I am burning
For the world to see
Unique and defiant
This is me
Aware
I am vocal
May these passions scream
Unafraid
To be silenced
For my words to reach
Yet invisible
In these pages
That I only
Read
A burned
Creation
No one will see

Extinguished
_hydrus

I want to find myself on your lips
And lose myself in your soul
_hydrus

Wounded the temple
You helped to build
Destroyed with intention
Demolished with skill

Risen this symbol
Broken in spite
Collapsing for reasons
Ones judgment incites

Always the victim
Walls shatter and fall
Lost in your rubble
Vacant my calls

False the foundation
On lies it was built
Selfish construction
Owned by your guilt

Property
_hydrus

Your eyes
In that moment
Gave me
What I could not see
In a lifetime
Seized by your stare
You saw my sadness
And all that was real
Behind a veil
Of insecurity and fear
You found my truth
We found each other
I found myself

Found
_hydrus

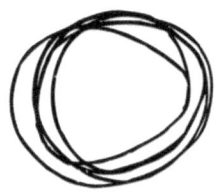

The skies opened up
Brought me to you
A morning star dressed
In celestial hues

I was the sunset
Dimmed in the light
Adorned by the shadows
A simple crescents knight

Endless were the days
Where moons dream of the sun
Together we will reign
But never just as one

Coupled
_hydrus

I should have
Held your hand
Reminded you
I was here
Sharing all the good
Wiping every tear
I should have been
Your light
A constant
Voice of faith
Urging every moment
Guiding every pace
I should have been your rock
Supporting
Every fall
Always have your back
Always at your call
I should have been
Yours

Reality
_hydrus

You went away
As oblivion roars
Found an escape
My heart simply ignores

Never to return
Broken as I stand
Lifes cruel simple
I am a vanquished man

Sudden
_hydrus

Sharpened teeth bleed
Within me they fed
Devoured my soul
Drank from my head

Left me to die
Yet juices still flowed
Now drained in this state
Inside you I grow

Digested
_hydrus

She traced every vein

knowing he bled for her

hydrus

Day still mourns
My distant ship
Never sailing
A dormant wick

An unknown voyage
Sands lay still
Unhealing questions
Against your will

Why must we lose
To gain our faith
Hidden emotions
Replaced by space

A clouded storm
Will blindly cast
Burn the canvas
Doubt your mast

Tides will drench
Life then drowns
My course now set
I am upside down
    Drifting
    _hydrus

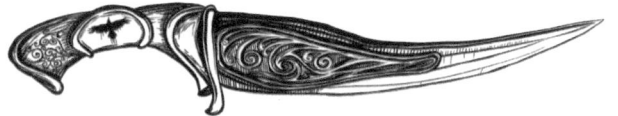

Happiness has deserted
Left a hole for all to see
Mocking every syllable
Reclaiming sadness with ease

Those who watch and wonder
Eagerly are quick to please
Undressing their hidden scabbards
Slicing what is left of me

Voyeurs
_hydrus

Impossible was leaving you
Incredible was that I did
Now you can starve
Let your crumbs
Be the only memory
No one remembers

Drowned
_hydrus

Live today as if there was no tomorrow
Tomorrow will soon be a distant yesterday

Live
_hydrus

Lonesome moonlight
Yearning to be loved
Voiceless anticipation
Judgement from above

Suddenly forgotten
Craving a simple kiss
Eagerly awaiting
Quietly dismissed

Sunset
_hydrus

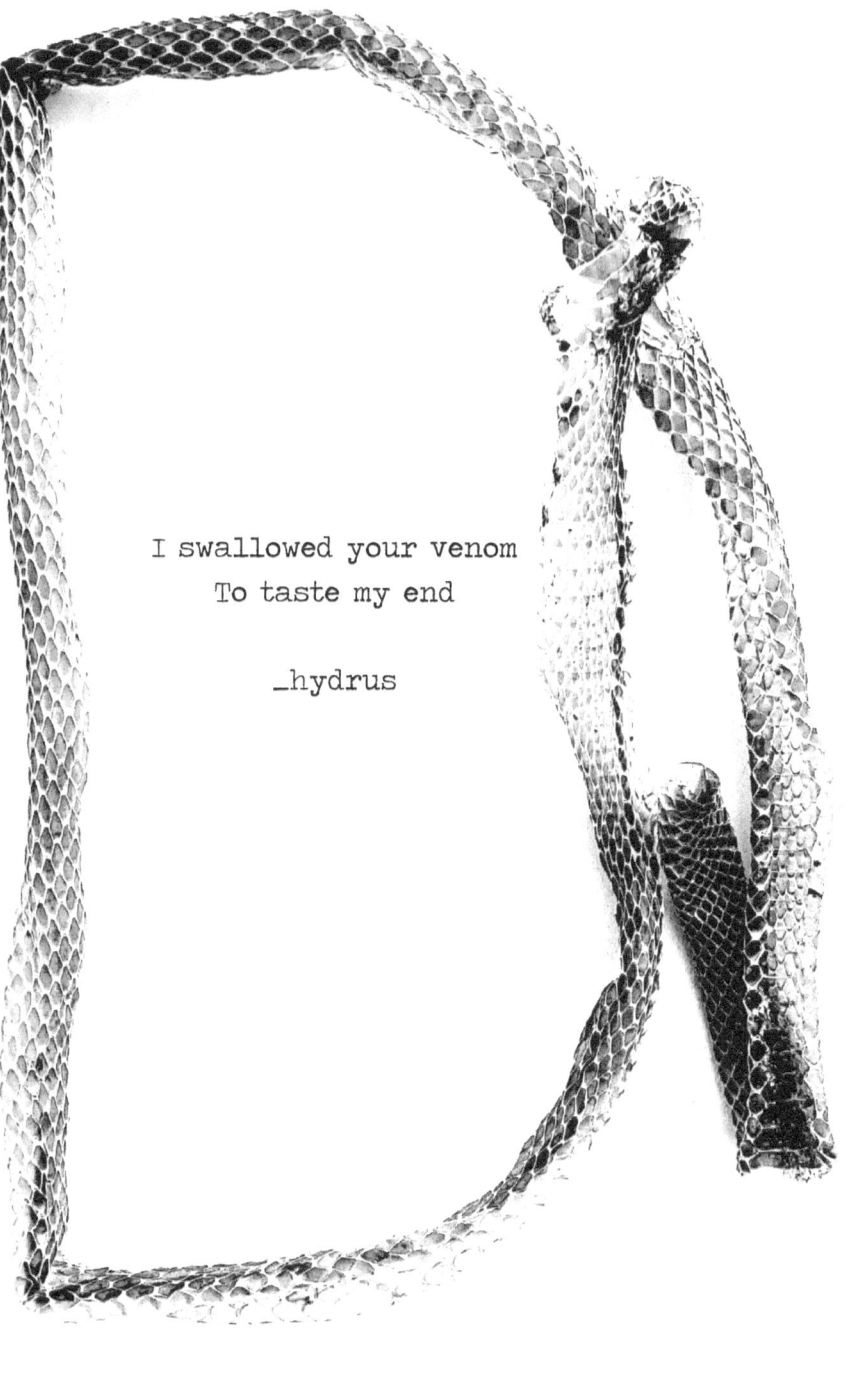

I swallowed your venom
To taste my end

_hydrus

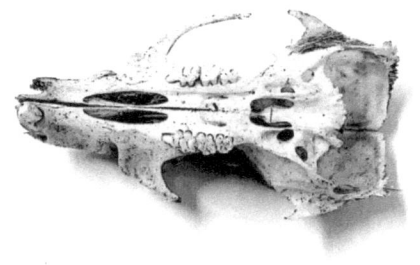

Tied by the ropes
You fastened with my fear
Sequestered by your lies
Vacant hopes just disappear

Reason has lost meaning
Subtle torture tightly bounds
Neatly you prepare me
Knotted present for the ground

Locked
_hydrus

Caressing phantom
Gentle to brush
Conjuring and waiting
Illusionary touch

Tender a witness
Hidden in the light
Quietly peering
Muted your plight

Kind are the whispers
Filling up my dreams
Feelings remembered
Emotions redeemed

Twilight embraces
Stolen my scars
Inside me you weep
Loved from so far

Searching
_hydrus

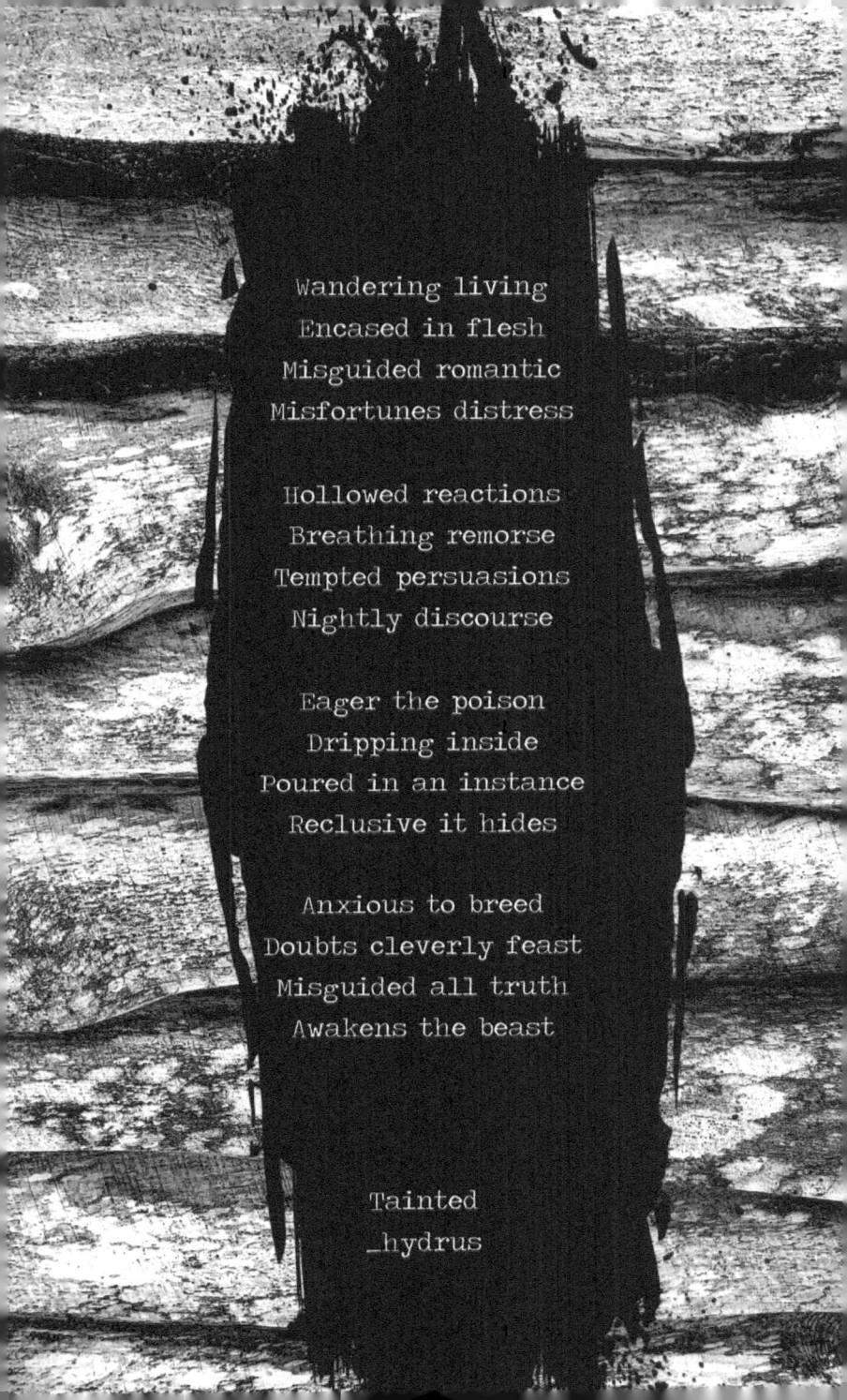

Wandering living
Encased in flesh
Misguided romantic
Misfortunes distress

Hollowed reactions
Breathing remorse
Tempted persuasions
Nightly discourse

Eager the poison
Dripping inside
Poured in an instance
Reclusive it hides

Anxious to breed
Doubts cleverly feast
Misguided all truth
Awakens the beast

Tainted
_hydrus

In darkness you wither
Worlds seem to fail
Peoples words linger
Expressed in betrayal

Alone one must feel
To endure such a fate
Often we falter
Sometimes just too late

Mirrors can judge
Voices may scream
Foggy the hope
Pulling the seams

Be brave to believe
In you there is light
Lonesome the vision
Internal the fight

My heart understands
The desire for love
Please hold my hand
Lets rise above

Reflect
_hydrus

Valleys drown in sorrow
As the winds declare defeat
Vacant stares are borrowed
Loss resides beneath

Infected minds are soured
Fortunes tell of their demise
Within us lives no morrow
Sadness blurs our tainted eyes

Storms
_hydrus

You took your
feather from my wings
Just to see me fall

_hydrus

Windows paint
Crying skies
Secrets faint
Vanished lies

Sinking thoughts
Single breaths
Floating souls
Empty rest

Broken hearts
Silent stares
Dormant walks
Unaware

Hidden secrets
Watchful eyes
New romance
Unspoken lives

Passing on
Shadows live
Inside your soul
I will live

Unwelcome
_hydrus

Fingers trace
Every moan
Body clenched
Sweaty groans

Tender lips
Soft caress
Panting kiss
Beaded breasts

Lavish scent
Drained of sin
Warm licks
On tender skin

Whispered treats
On bedded silk
Hardened veins
Quenched in milk

Wrapping legs
Mounting bones
Selfish acts
All alone

Divine
_hydrus

Sun bathes her body
Waves embracing shapes
Slowly fingers searching
Longing for escape

Ripples dance on waves
Sand caressing skin
Washing sins in sight
Burying cravings within

Carnal winds arouse
Constantly yearning to take
Our flame never burns out
Destiny found us too late

Stranded
_hydrus

Magic walls
Built on lies
Captured visions
In disguise

Ruptured violence
Tattered scenes
Unwilling virtues
Unforeseen

Captive native
Clawing doors
Unrelenting
On all fours

Crying yelping
Gasping air
Tortured presence
In despair

Call the crows
End this pain
Help me shadows
Break my chains

Mired
_hydrus

Misguided roads
Lead me here
A twisted journey
Full of fear

Unpaved equations
I never missed
A hopeful union
An ungodly bliss

Trenches came
I overturned
Hollow fiction
Engulfed I burned

Now on my way
My memories wane
Reckless nights
I lay afraid

Longing road
That bends astray
With no direction
The demons play

Descended
_hydrus

Tortured Light
Burning just to burn
Ignoring your sight
Hypnotic concern

A faded scent
Flickering just to flick
Directionless might
Motives so sick

Dwindling plight
Living just to live
Extinguished your fight
I will never forgive

Dimmed
_hydrus

My hands found meaning
When she placed them on herself

_hydrus

Quiet the shell
That once held my hand
A loving life taken
By the grains in the sand

Linear points etched
In the oceanless sky
Left my heart empty
The moment you died

Never forgotten
The child you held
A gift to the builder
So many stories to tell

A ship has now sailed
Your seas are now calm
Encased in my sorrow
Are the lines you left drawn

Sail
_hydrus

Laughter buries
Unemotional acts
Of antics untold
Love that now lacks

Hearts once ablaze
Scorching all earth
Now dim in existence
Extinguished the torch

Desperate in hunger
Needs mourn as they beg
Reluctant to eat
Craving to bed

Yet the fire still flames
Unknown to who jests
This body still yearns
It awaits to ingest

Longing
_hydrus

Jagged the guilt
That severed your head
Bewildered and topless
Reluctant you bled

Payments conceived
Anguish withdrawn
Slaughtered in life
Reaped to not spawn

Payback
_hydrus

Sculpted angel
Etched in tears
Frozen wings
Chiseled fear

Arched encryptions
Carved with pain
Eroded hopes
Posed in vain

Muted cries
Adorned in stone
Contoured dreams
Fainted moans

Encased seclusion
Built on lies
Admired sadness
Life denied

Unveiled
_hydrus

Idiots will dance
To a foolish song
A fumbling trance
When all goes wrong

Unknown confusion
Trick the fool
Awakened conclusions
Remotely cruel

Sadness paints
The solemn clown
Reality awaits
A lasting frown

All the magic and
Spells have worn
A dimmed light
Is left to mourn

The Show
_hydrus

Alone I drown
In what never was
Saddened scars
Falling drops

Punctured heart
Faded thoughts
Ripped apart
No new start

Words defy
Unspoken myths
Faint betrayal
A twisted gift

Defeated story
Washed ashore
A fabled jester
Loved no more

Wrecked
_hydrus

I can't fix
What I didn't break
It wasn't mine
One couldn't wait

They aren't here
We shouldn't be
I mustn't fear
Who isn't me

Won't
_hydrus

I only
breathe
the memories
of what
we were

_hydrus

Fingers speak
Of a dripping pain
A sleepless night
Alone again

Wishful thoughts
Spawn to dream
Relived with sorrow
Unwanted streams

Haunted sights
Plague the soul
Truthful lies
Take their toll

In my sky
The stars will flee
A darkened sun
Left for me

Dusk
_hydrus

Troubled the beast
That sits in his cave
Conjuring an image
Of a distant rampage
The moment he slept
Hunters came for their skins
Gutted and thrusted
Their weapons with grins
Foolish he waits
As the moon takes the stars
Pains are too great
Far deep run the scars
Tomorrow will bring
Another night so unclear
Too tired and spent
Misled by ones spear

Wounded
_hydrus

Laughing crows
Fly my way
Approach my state
In its decay

They perch to stare
Poke in haste
Peck my sins
Beg to taste

Tear my skin
Inside they feast
A bloodied heart
They quickly eat

Once consumed
Again they fly
Leave my bones
Where I lie

cavenged
hydrus

I wake from sleep
Still I mourn
The days still blur
Ruined by storms

The pounding rain
Inside grows deaf
A willingness
To never rest

Shelters built
Pierced by stones
An angry wind
Forever moans

Its deafening roar
A loss of faith
Reclaiming tears
I cannot face

Thrown
_hydrus

A single print
Erased in sand
Alone again
I understand

Not enough
A distant choice
Wondering doubts
Exploited noise

Homeless heart
Left to bleed
Bring the tide
I will retreat

Swept
_hydrus

To feel the sunlight
Off the blades of grass
A childish abstract
That reminds the past

Rendered scenes
Of unbridled care
Warm delusions
Worlds so unaware

Meadows canvassed
With a foggy brush
Hide the thorns
Snaring the rush

For if you nap
In this splendid field
Confessed flowers
Will unmask your shield

Poisoned
_hydrus

Scars performed
By blinded time
Insides devoured
Hidden the crimes

Unknowns relived
A vivid play
Reactions cringe
To a danced display

Notes in sweat
Flow through flesh
Songs in heat
Undress distress

Tales then told
To ease all pain
Final the curtain
A love now stained

Act
_hydrus

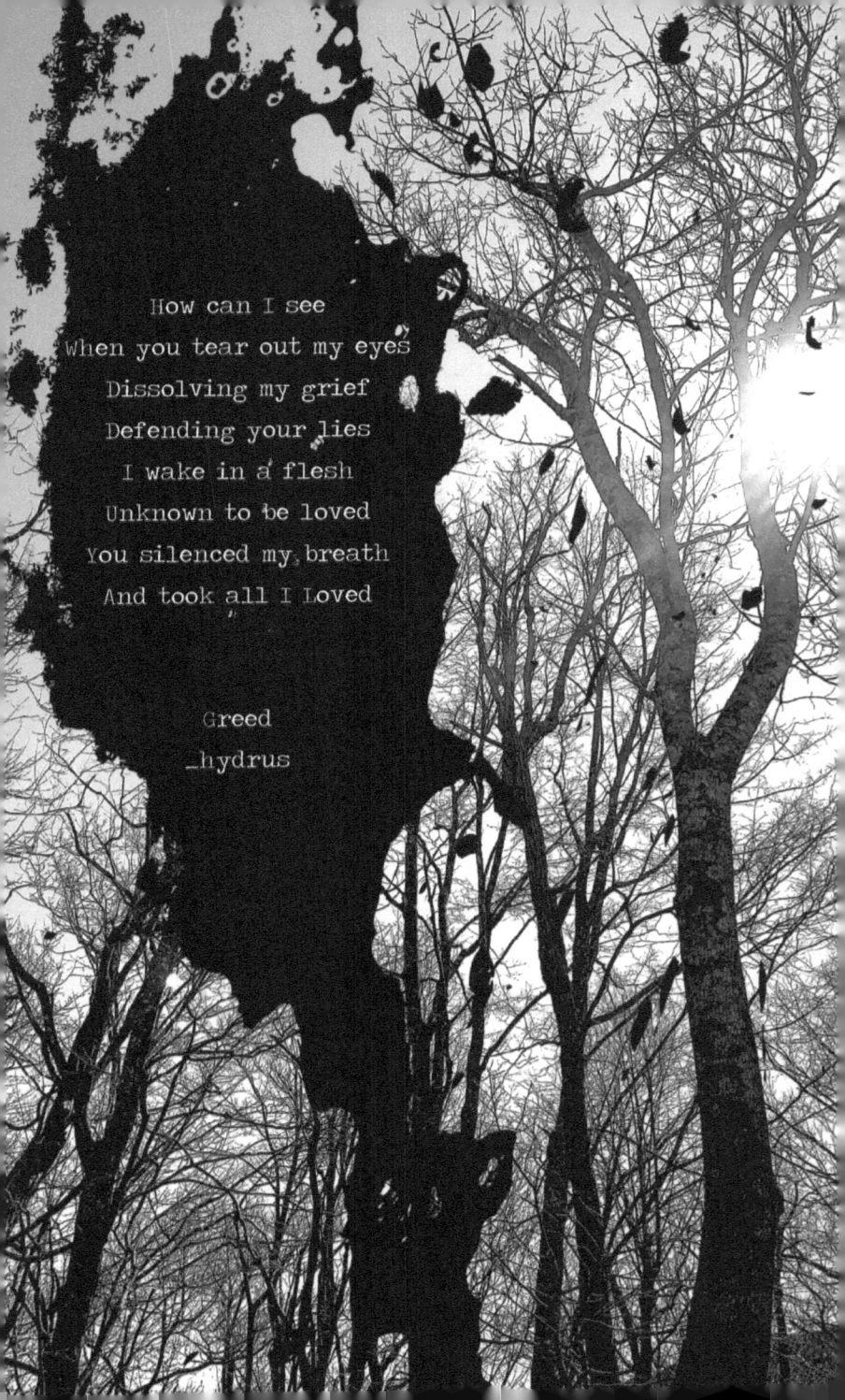

How can I see
When you tear out my eyes
Dissolving my grief
Defending your lies
I wake in a flesh
Unknown to be loved
You silenced my breath
And took all I Loved

Greed
_hydrus

When you left
I adopted
Your demons
Nurtured
And made them
My own
They are angrily
Famished
With hunger
In your nightmares
I let them
Go home

Cradle
_hydrus

I only sleep
So I can dream of her

_hydrus

Perished stones
Tainted gloom
Lined in unison
Adorning tombs

Rocks and earth
Below they wait
Famished worms
Will investigate

Bone and skin
Arrive to nest
Laced in blood
Dressed in their best

Spectered tales
Begin to rise
Returned to haunt
With waning cries

Darkness looms
Inside us all
Timeless tomb
Will bury us all

Fatal
_hydrus

For You
I will slowly wait
To bed the darkness
That blends my shape
Gently
I will taste
The fiery cauldron
Below your waste

Again
_hydrus

Fragmented thoughts
Cloud my sense
Of a love birthed
With no pretense
Unimagined souls
A joy defined
An everlasting trance
When you were mine
Broken the chalice
One held in light
Slaughtered in thought
An impending night
All hope consumed
Quenched by guilt
Forgotten union
When blood was spilled

Crumble
_hydrus

Absent the figure
Who hovers so clear
A shadow above me
Observing my fear

Cowered and frozen
It peers in my eyes
Awakened to sleep
As I watch myself die

Collected
_hydrus

Her hands
Held me
As if we were
Alone
My eyes
Deceived her
I was never
Hers to own
Betrayed amusement
Never to forget
The pain
Enlightens
Just a lost regret

Forgotten
_hydrus

I want to be the only sin you taste

_hydrus

Languished feelings
Ignite my sores
Secret dealings
Such rancid whores

Weakness blushes
Owed fate expires
Looming crushes
Pungent denials

A sharpened blade
Awaits to taste
Bitter dealings
Of forbidden mates

For when the skin
Secretes all pain
Impaled with sin
Blood will paint their shame

Earned
_hydrus

I cannot remember a day
In which breathing
Did not begin
Without the thought
Of you.

Living
_hydrus

Pale white flesh
Hexed in stone
Black filled lips
Skull and bones

A covens chant
Burned to please
Fluid dances
Brewed and teased

Cursed ghosts
Haunt the moon
Enchanted minxes
Drink their groom

Thirsty muses
Crackled laughs
Muttered spells
In seductive baths

Wiccans tale
A casted prey
Drunk on madness
I must obey

Cleansed
_hydrus

Singed imperfection
A dragonflies wings
Sequestered immortality
Lit to unhinge

Slow infidelity
Drinking my poor
A warning shot cast
Wealth will absorb

Lost in my sequence
My valley I scaled
Defined by experience
Humanity impaled

Later
_hydrus

Branded thieves
Waste away
Inside themselves
Tuned to prey

Crippled teeth
Slaughtered eyes
Wretched taste
A cowards lies

Upon their mask
They lay in wait
Abused defiance
Neglected hate

Wraths will tell
Tombs are scribed
Hell awaits
Souls will dine

Blazed
_hydrus

My thorns became your muse
Your words became my cross
_hydrus

Through the chimney
Spied the caws
Inside its grasp
Hearts were raw

Tattered fool
In delusions ear
Without regrets
Awaiting jeers

Muted the air
Wings left the perch
Time beckoned breath
A pulsating search

On its return
It cried again
Reminding me
That all must end

Finally
_hydrus

Drunk in a taxicab
Preaching memories
Ashed cigarettes
Amused at the trees

Bathtub of lies
Iced in descent
Soap cannot cleanse
My evils wont repent

Debris
_hydrus

Patterned repetition
Incredible melt
An educated idiot
Serrated it felt

A trilogy of failure
Flavored and ripped
Knowing you are last
workshop ill equipped

Alien in motto
New orders to obey
Forgotten evolution
A memory I evade

Tragic
_hydrus

Bleeding echoes
Frightening plea
Tattooed crosses
Mayhems effigy

Prescribed addiction
Nocturnal rale
Failed conclusion
Embed your nails

Mutilate
_hydrus

Fit of rage
Why do you care
Emboldened demons
Live out despair

Fame not granted
A public ghost
In a borrowed life
Inside you roast

Inadequate
_hydrus

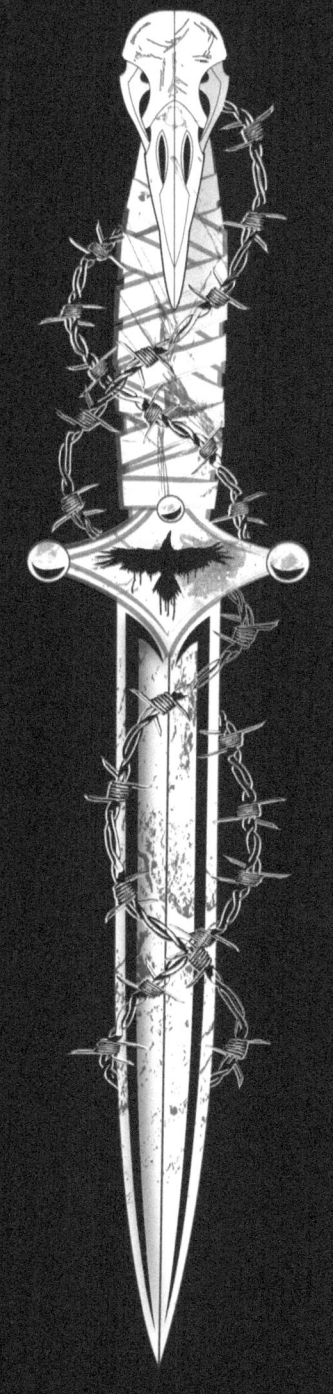

Time defines
Who we are
Its a tiny glimpse
From our distant star

A morning memory
Where routines begin
Losing ourselves
Playing out our sins

Wrapped in chaos
Slaves to our ways
So much emotion
To each doubted day

The serpents toil
Yet we are gone
Our souls rewritten
Our lives move on

END
_hydrus

Thank You

To all my readers
for all your love and support.
It means the world to me
and inspires me to keep bleeding…

Thank you to all my Ravens!
You continuously amaze me
with your love, devotion, and curiosity.
Your overall openness to venture with me
wherever the ink guides us is truly humbling
and always very heartwarming.

...And of course Thank You to
Cleo at @devoted_pages
For all of her endless support, hard work, time
and energy that she puts into making all of my
darkness look so beautiful.

The boundaries which divide Life from Death
are at best shadowy and vague.
Who shall say where the one ends,
and where the other begins?

Edgar Allan Poe

Also by _hydrus

ENDVISIBLE

A collection of poems about the endless feeling of being invisible while going through the emotions and sometimes cruelties of life. Illustrated by the author's own photography, this book guides us through grief, loss and love in a dark and inspiring way typical to how Hydrus's writing helps us cope with reality.

AWAKEND

Tarots cards, much like poems, have the ability to paint a vivid picture of what once was or what could be. They delve into the subtleties that we all carry within ourselves and the secrets that make us who we are.

AwakEND is an immersion into the world of tarot and its mysteries. Read it one way, then another, and let the words guide you into the meaning of each card. Allow chance and curiosity to accompany you on this incredible journey and let your heart awaken to hope even after having thought everything was lost...

And who knows what secrets you might find out about yourself...

DARK**END**

Is a small look into the world I call my reality.
Through poems, photography and art, I try to capture the ups and downs of this
voyage we call life, and sometimes I refer to it as just existing.
Embedded in my words are stories of emotions and feelings that range from the
darkest of moments to times of having some type of hope for resolve.

Life is raw and ever-evolving, and we always seem to put ourselves last over-
all. Time proves to be quite relentless. I hope that we all find common ground
through our everyday struggles and in the end, understand that love, although
painful at times, can provide so many answers.

So the question then becomes *"how can we better love ourselves?"*

HEART**END**

Is about how we experience love and some of the journeys we embark on
when love strikes our heart. It's about the numerous complex phases and ever
changing stages of the purest human emotions.
It might be a first kiss, a new romance, a guilty pleasure or a sense of loss but
love always helps us reach the heavens or crash down upon its shores.
Love gives even when it takes,
it heals and embeds its mark and sculpts us into who we are.

"We all open our hearts and in the end this is the love we bleed." *_hydrus*

About The Author

Anonymous poet, photographer and artist,
Hydrus documents through his poems the darkness and the
glimmers of life taunting us when we are in the shadows,
as well as many of the little things which make a colossal impact
on who we are.

Connect with _hydrus:

Website: www.hydruspoetry.com
Instagram: @hydruspoetry
Facebook: www.facebook.com/hydruspoetry
Redbubble Merchandise:
www.redbubble.com/people/hydruspoetry/explore

Write Your Soul

_hydrus

www.ingramcontent.com/pod-product-compliance
Lightning Source LLC
Chambersburg PA
CBHW030905080526
44589CB00010B/161